ESMONT VIRGINIA

*A Community Carved from the Earth
and Sustained by Story*

ESMONT VIRGINIA

*A Community Carved from the Earth
and Sustained by Story*

**FRIENDS OF ESMONT
WITH ANDI CUMBO-FLOYD**

Esmont, Virginia
Copyright ©2020 Friends of Esmont

Published by Andilit

Cover image:
Esmont National Bank (Photograph by Eduardo Montes-Bradley, CC BY-SA 4.0 license, https://commons.wikimedia.org/w/index.php?curid=52339284)

Cover by Stephanie Spino
Book Design by James Woosley (FreeAgentPress.com)

ISBN: 9781952430084 (print)
ISBN: 9781952430091 (e-book)

For Lucille Purvis Goff,
Esmont's leading lady.

Lucille Purvis Goff
(Photograph by Peggy Purvis Denby, Friends of Esmont)

CONTENTS

Foreword ix

Esmont Community Time Line xi

Introduction 1

Early Inhabitants 3

    Monacan Settlements 5

Land Grants – Eighteenth and Nineteenth Centuries 9

    Land Grants 10

Plantations 15

    The Coleses' Plantations 17

    Canaan Plantation (now known as Liberty Corner) 21

    Mount Warren Plantation 21

    Esmont Plantation 23

    Other Plantations in Esmont 25

Villages **27**

Churches **29**

 Ballenger Church 29

 Mount Zion Methodist Church 33

 Sharon Baptist Church 34

 New Hope Baptist Church 35

 Chestnut Grove Baptist Church 35

 Mount Alto Baptist Church 37

 Sand Road Baptist Church 38

 New Green Mountain Baptist Church 38

 Saint Stephen's Episcopal Church 39

Schools **41**

Industry **49**

Commerce **61**

 Porter's Precinct 62

 Esmont Village 66

Epilogue **73**

A Note from Friends of Esmont **75**

About the Author **79**

Acknowledgements **81**

Notes **85**

FOREWORD

WHEN **I** BEGAN RESTORING Esmont in 1999, I wasn't just bringing back a house that master architectural historian, Ed Lay, called "perfect." I was also bringing back, at least for me, a period in time—the washpots and flapping clotheslines in the side yard, the smell of ham frying in the summer kitchen, the laughter in the high-ceilinged rooms, the sorrow and desperation as well as the triumphs of the enslaved population.

My architect and I left the char on the beams in the smokehouse, used the handmade doors in the basement, with their numerous keyholes and latches, and allowed degrading plaster walls in the summer kitchen to remain as they were, with plantation-made brick showing through.

I once walked across the yard near the old kitchen and smelled food cooking. It was a calming and happy fragrance, diffused into the open autumn air. It quickened my blood, because trust me, there was no food cooking on the property that day. Yet spirit answers to spirit, heart speaks to heart, and across the span of nearly two hundred years, there can be tender connections.

Rehabbing and renovating have their satisfactions, but loving restoration trumps it all. How else would I have learned that the mortar in the walls leading to the attic contained human hair, horsehair, apple pollen, and spores of tuberculosis? How else would I have known that a front-door key can weigh a pound and a half and be worn around the neck on a ribbon if circumstances demand?

You may find extensive archives, on the house, the village, and the people, in Special Collections at the Alderman Library of the University of Virginia, including a restored set of nine volumes of farm journals kept faithfully by William Gordon, son-in-law of Esmont's first owner, Dr. Charles Cocke.

Jan Karon
Esmont 1999-2014

ESMONT COMMUNITY TIME LINE

5000 BC   Monacan presence in Esmont, particularly
          in relation to soapstone repositories, from
          which they carved ceremonials bowls.

1730   Francis Eppes received land grant: 6,500
          acres that would become Alberene and most of
          Green Mountain area to north of Plank Rd.

~1747   Enniscorthy Plantation established by Coles family.

1748   Thomas McDaniel received land grant: 350 acres
          that would become Esmont Plantation and Village.

1750   Matthew Jordan received land grant: 324
          acres that would become Porter's Precinct.

1750   Ballenger Church founded.

1750   Morrisena Farm built.

1765   River Lawn Plantation built.

1780   Mount Warren Plantation built for Wilson Cary Nicholas.

1784	Rezin Porter received land grant from king of England: 450 acres that would sit both west and east of current-day Esmont.
1785	Seven Oaks Plantation built by Benjamin Childress.
1785	Canaan Plantation (now Liberty Corner) established for Harris family.

Current house built around 1835 |
| 1789 | Enniscorthy Plantation house built.

Burned in 1839. |
1789	Wingfield Place built.
1762	The glebe farm built for Saint Anne's Parish (Langhorne Rd.).
1796	Woodville built for Walter Coles.
1800	Calycanthus Hill house built at location of current Estouteville.
1803	Tallwood built.
1806	Donegal Plantation built.
1814	Rezin Porter sold Charles Cocke 1184 acres on and along Green Mountain.
1816	Esmont Plantation house built.
1827	Estouteville Plantation house built.
1828	Mount Zion Methodist Church log meetinghouse built.
1850	Current Enniscorthy Plantation house built.
1852	Sharon Baptist Church founded.
1853	Monticola Plantation house built for Daniel James Hartsook.
1855	Warren Store built.
1865	New Hope Baptist Church formed.
1867	Porter's Precinct appeared on Hotchkiss map.
1868	Chestnut Grove Baptist Church formed.
1869	Glendower Freedman's School opened.
1874	First school for Black children started.

1878	Log school for Black children built on land donated by John Lane.
1882	Mount Alto Baptist Church founded.
1883	Beaver Dam Farm purchased by James Serene for soapstone quarry.
1883	Sand Road Baptist Church founded.
1884	Alberene quarry opened.
1890	Original Mount Alto School built.
1892	Virginia Soapstone began in Schuyler.
1892	New Woodville house built.
1895	Alberene Railroad incorporated.
1896	New Green Mountain Baptist Church formed.
1898	Alberene Railroad opened.
~1898	Nydrie built.
1899	Carbolane slate quarry opened in Esmont. Closed by 1910.
~1900	School for Black students began at Loving Charity Lodge on Porters Rd.
1900	Butler/Purvis Store opened.
1901	Schuyler Railway opened.
1901	Guthrie Hall built.
1902	Esmont National Bank opened. Closed in 1933.
1903	Nelson and Albemarle Railway construction began.
~1903	Coleswood house built.
1904	Albemarle Soapstone and Virginia Soapstone merged.
1905	Hilltop School built.
1906	Nelson and Albemarle Railway opened.
1906	Black men formed School League.
1907	Women's Educational League formed from Black community.
1907	Grand United Order of Odd Fellows Hall opened.

1907   Steed's Store opened.

1908   Esmont Inn opened in village.

1908   School for Black children opened at the Loving Charity Lodge/W. D. Ward Community Center (now the Odd Fellows Hall).

1909   Last quarry closed at Alberene.

1910   Chestnut Grove School opened.

1911   Lane company store opened.

Burned down in 1996.

1912   Educational Board of Esmont deeded county 3 acres for school on land that would eventually hold B. F. Yancey Elementary School.

1914   Saint Stephen's Episcopal Church founded.

1915   Thomas's Store in Porter's Precinct opened.

1915   Esmont Colored School opened.

1916   Alberene mill closed.

1916   Virginia Alberene Corporation formed.

650 men employed.

1920   Rebuilt Mount Alto School opened.

1922   Esmont Elementary School for White students opened.

1924   Alberoyd Company of Esmont formed.

1925   1,000 employed at 35 quarries in Esmont area.

1930   Pace's Store opened.

1934   Schuyler mill closed.

~1935   "Little School" opened for Black K–4th grade students, and Esmont High School took over for Colored School, educating 5th–11th graders.

1935   Bankrupt Virginia Alberene reorganized as Alberene Stone Corporation of Virginia.

~1940s PTA of Black community bought 4 more acres of land.

1944   Parent-Teacher League of Esmont High School, in the Black community, bought additional 4 acres, bringing the total to 7 acres for high school on Porters Rd.

1944 Floods destroyed Nelson and Albemarle Railway
       track between Schuyler and Rockfish.

       Track then legally abandoned in 1947.

1957 Quarrying at Alberene resumed.

1957 Blue Ridge Slate closed due to dust (on order of the state).

1960 B. F. Yancey Elementary School opened.

       Closed by county in 2017.

1962 Nelson and Albemarle Railway line abandoned.

1963 Esmont Inn burned.

1964 Esmont Depot demolished.

1978 Esmont Health Center (now Southern
       Albemarle Family Practice) began.

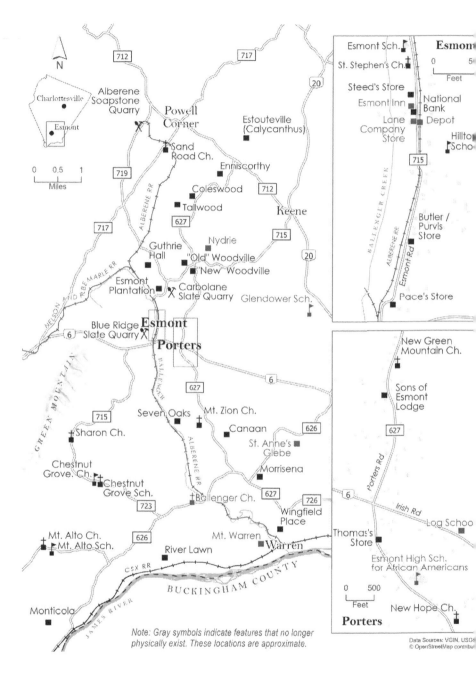

Historical locations around Esmont and Porter's
(Courtesy of Erik Irtenkauf)

INTRODUCTION

IN THE SOUTHWEST CORNER of Virginia's Albemarle County, a county known most widely for being the home of Thomas Jefferson and James Monroe, a quiet community has been thriving far longer than those two men were president, much longer even than they were alive. This quiet place now goes by the name of Esmont, but before that it was called Porter's Precinct and Chestnut Grove and, before that, the land of the Monacans.

Now, in the early twenty-first century, the community is made up of rural but deeply interconnected communities of people whose roots go back generations in that soapstone and slate-rich soil. The country roads are lined with small houses, an occasional plantation house of brick rising on a hillside.

Along the largest road, a few stores offer gasoline and soda to neighbors and passersby, and on the smaller thruways, the storefronts of a century-old heyday stand tribute to the hard work and long commitment of owners and customers alike.

Esmont, Virginia, is a community deep in history and rich in connection, and in that, it is like many a rural locale in the United States. But in another way, it is like those locations as well—it is entirely its own presence and carries on a unique story that is only true here, in these few square miles of land.

Some writers have characterized this place as poor or abandoned, a zombie town even, but those people lacked the vision to see the truth of this spot—that it is vibrant and complex, beloved and beholden to the people who call it home.

If you venture into this place through the pages of this book, you will find an Esmont that provided the materials for sacred objects and for big industry, an Esmont riven and rich with the history and legacy of slavery and the people shaped by that horrible institution, a place of families and ancestors, and a place still very much living, well, and restoring itself into more of what it has always been.

From the Monacans who first settled on this land to the plantation owners and enslaved people they brought with them, to the industry tycoons who built quarries and railroads, to the business owners and educators who provided for their families and their neighbors, and on to the descendants who live in the legacy of their ancestors even as they create their own legacies to pass on, Esmont tells a story for us all. A story of resilience and rootedness. A story of hope.

EARLY INHABITANTS

MONACAN
SETTLEMENTS

THE HUMAN HISTORY OF the place we now know as Esmont began back before history was written down but when it was nevertheless very much happening in the lives of the Native American people of the area, the Monacans. The Monacans lived in and traveled through this part of Virginia at least as early as 10,000 BC and still have a presence in nearby Amherst County, the site they now consider their tribal home.

The earliest Monacans were a traveling people, migrating through the Central Virginia region as resources and trading with other groups necessitated. The Monacans spent significant time in the Esmont area, mining the soapstone that is so abundant.

The stone has been a core resource through centuries in Southern Albemarle, but the first to understand the stone's value were the Monacans. From roughly 4000 to 1000 BC, Monacan artisans harvested soapstone from the repositories that run through Nelson and Albemarle counties.

Archaeologist David I. Bushnell visited the area in the early twentieth century and observed more than twenty trace pits where Monacan people had harvested soapstone for use in their ceremonial vessels. He also took note of numerous partial or broken and discarded bowls that had been damaged in the production process, and finished bowls still exist today as testaments to the mastery of the carvers who shaped them.

Ceremonial bowl
(Courtesy of the Tracy W. McGregor Library of American History,
Albert and Shirley Small Special Collections Library,
University of Virginia Library, Charlottesville, Virginia)

These objects were quite large and heavy, so heavy that it might take an adult two hands to simply drag them. As noted by Michael Klein, an archaeology PhD student at the University of Virginia,

> the vessel form, the social import of soapstone exchange, and ethnographic observation of the use of similar vessels for stone boiling and serving of meats, fishes and ritual tea indicate that these bowls are better suited for processing those items most likely consumed during rituals, or for serving ritual drinks or foods, than for generalized cooking. The morphological similarity and widespread exchange of soapstone vessels indicate a pan regional ritual activity linked by exchange ties.[1]

Such items, quarried from stone in Esmont, were used throughout the region because of the networks of exchange that the Monacans developed as part of their tribal economic system.

Around AD 1000 the Monacan people became agricultural and more settled, establishing communities on the floodplains of the Virginia Piedmont's rivers like the James, Rappahannock, Rivanna, and Rapidan.[2] At the time the Monacans encountered the first Europeans in Virginia, from Jamestown in 1608, there were more than ten thousand people in the Monacan confederacy; and by the end of that century, there were many towns, including Rassawek, in their territory, which ranged from the Piedmont into the mountains of Virginia.[3]

English colonist John Smith learned the names of five of the many Monacan settlements on the James: Mowhemcho, Massinacack, Rassawek, Monahassanough (possibly near Wingina), and Monasukapanough on the south fork of the Rivanna River.

While none of these were specifically in the Esmont area, we can assume that Monacan people traveling between Rassawek and Monahassanough, in particular, would have regularly traversed the lands near Warren and Howardsville and further north into the areas of Alberene and Schuyler, where the soapstone deposits were most rich. This land in Southern Albemarle was part of their territory for more than ten thousand years.

Thus, the Monacan people have long held deep ties to the land of what we now call Esmont. They incorporated its resources into not only their daily lives but also into the ceremonies and rituals that held particular importance and power in their culture, and they called this land home for eons, far longer than any other group of people yet to live there.

Their connection to this place is deep, long, and very much alive, even if their principal place of residence now is a bit further south and west, in Amherst County.

LAND GRANTS
– EIGHTEENTH AND NINETEENTH CENTURIES

ALTHOUGH THE MONACAN PEOPLE had been calling the region we now know as Southern Albemarle part of their homeland for centuries, the process of colonization did not honor that fact. When the first Europeans arrived on this continent, they considered these lands "available" for settlement by both England and the newly formed United States of America, despite the Native American inhabitants.

To claim this land for king and country and to formally displace the Native Americans living or traveling here, the English Crown established a system of distributing title to the land of Virginia, their newly formed colony. Typically, this process goes by the term "land grant system."

Land Grants

After settlers first arrived in Jamestown and prior to the Revolutionary War, land was allocated through a system that was administered by the colonial government on behalf of the English monarch. Through that system, individuals were awarded tracts of land based on the number of people they funded for passage to the colonies. Thus, the more people someone brought to the "new world," the more access that settler had to land.

This process is often referred to as the "headright system." For example, if a person brought himself, his wife, three children, and sixteen slaves, he could be awarded 1,050 acres of land in the colony's "unappropriated or waste territory."[4]

The second system of land grants came into effect after the United States declared its independence from England and reflects more of the standard practice of purchasing land that we know now—except, of course, no individual held title to these lands at that time, and therefore land was considered "unappropriated." To purchase unappropriated land, a person paid £40 for one hundred acres (approximately $7,300 in current American dollars).[5] No limits were placed on the amount of land an individual could purchase.

In the area of southern Albemarle County that incorporates the communities of Chestnut Grove, Porter's Precinct, and Esmont Village, three men were given land grants under the first system.

- Matthew Jordan received 324 acres on June 1, 1750, and his land rested on the area surrounding the crossroads of what are now Irish Road and Porters Road.

- Abraham Eades received a grant for 160.5 acres on September 20, 1755, and his land included what is now the very southern end of Esmont Village and south across Irish Road.
- Thomas McDaniel received his grant for 350 acres, and his land incorporated what is now Esmont Village, spanning both east and west of present-day Esmont Road.

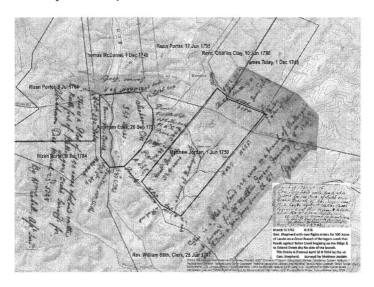

Land grants
(Courtesy of Bob Vernon)

One additional individual who purchased land in the Porter's Precinct/Chestnut Grove/Esmont Village area in 1795 would leave his mark on the community for posterity. That man was Rezin Porter, who acquired over one thousand acres of land in three tracts across the area now considered Esmont.

11

- Porter's first tract spanned from the road that now carries his name, Porters Road, north to almost current-day Esmont Road.
- The second 400 acres was located west of Esmont Village and both north and south of what is now Irish Road.
- The final tract of 140 acres was adjacent to the previous one and incorporates what is now the northern part of Chestnut Grove Road.

Porter served as a surveyor of roads for the early US government, and it's likely this position is the reason the road that ran through his land was given his name.

However, Rezin Porter's time in Southern Albemarle was short. By 1812, he had moved southeast, to Prince Edward County, where he stayed until his death in 1820, and we have no further records of his presence in Esmont at all—just the road and the community that bear his name.

Additional land grants in the area were given to:
- John Jones,
- Francis Eppes (the grandson of Thomas Jefferson, Eppes owned the largest tract in the area, 6,500 acres on Green Mountain),
- Archibald McCollin,
- John Sneed,
- John Martin,
- Moses Martin,
- William Stith (first president of William & Mary),
- John Lewis,
- Ralph Thomas,
- Thomas Goolsby,

- James Skelton,
- Jacob Morris,
- John Scott,
- John Eads,
- James Tuley,
- Charles Clay,
- John Coles,
- Thomas Ogilsbe,
- and William Watkins.[6]

Many of these men and their descendants held places of high prominence in early Virginia society.

Under both systems of grantorship, the grantee needed to prove their right to the land—either through documentation of immigration or a receipt from the state treasury. Once that document was received, a surveyor was sent out to mark the metes and bounds of the said tract. The surveyor then came back to record the surveyed property as belonging to the individual who proved their right to obtain it.

It is these surveys that form the basis for the ownership of land that is still at work in Virginia today, and a diligent researcher could track a particular parcel of land in Esmont, say along Boatwright Lane in the village, all the way back to the first land grant. These trails of ownership often tell much of the story of a place like Esmont, where the history is written in families more than it is in books.

PLANTATIONS

ONCE LAND OWNERSHIP WAS established among the early European Americans in Albemarle County, the plantation system was able to take root fully. As the fundamental economic driver for much of the South in the eighteenth and nineteenth centuries, plantations and their accompanying system of slavery were the primary means to wealth and regard in early Virginia, and such was certainly the case in Esmont.

In southern Albemarle County, several prominent families—some with ties to the original land grants described above and some who purchased land from those original grantees—established plantations. In fact, in the early colonial period of American history, the most accurate description of the region we now call Esmont is to think of it as a series of interconnected plantation-based communities, a quilt of plantations if you will.

With the exception of Warren, towns did not yet exist in the area, and so most of the needs of the individuals living in this locale were met on the plantation itself or through a network of trade with other plantations; and trips to "town"—at the time Scottsville or Charlottesville—were very rare and only undertaken if they could not be avoided or if they accompanied a visit to friends or family for several days.

Consider that the distance from Esmont Village to Court Square in Charlottesville is twenty-eight miles, a day's ride on a horse. No one made that trip into town casually.

Thus, plantations provided as much as they could for those who lived on them—both White and Black people—or they worked with neighboring plantations for what they could not raise, grow, or craft themselves. Most plantations had vegetable gardens and livestock for goods such as milk, butter, eggs, and meat. Additionally, on most plantations of any size, enslaved laborers would do everything from work the fields to tend the animals, to spin thread and weave clothes, to also waiting on the enslavers' families as cooks, nurses, house servants, and drivers.

What couldn't be made, grown, or raised on a plantation would be bought or bartered for, sometimes from stores in places like Charlottesville or Richmond but more likely, if possible, from nearby plantations. For example, enslaved craftspeople made goods—everything from shoes to clothing to farming equipment—for trade or sale to other plantations.

Likewise, enslaved people were often hired out by their enslavers for labor at other plantations, particularly during seasons of heavy work, such as when a field might require ditching or a home or other structure was being built.

To grasp the social and economic network of early Virginia, we need to understand that people of that time worked largely to care for their own places and those who lived there. While some individuals had other kinds of work in professional capacities—attorneys like Patrick Henry or politicians such as Thomas Jefferson and James Madison—most plantation owners, like those in Esmont, were gentlemen farmers whose wealth came from their land and from the people they enslaved.

In appreciating Esmont as an early American community, then, we must recognize it as a quilt of plantations that included White and Black inhabitants who interacted with each other both socially and economically through and around the system of slavery.

The Coleses' Plantations

One of the earliest plantation owners in the Esmont area was John Coles (1705–1747), who purchased three thousand acres of land on Green Mountain from Francis Eppes's estate. There, Coles established a residence that his son John Coles II (1745–1805) inherited upon his father's death. In 1789, Coles II had the Enniscorthy Plantation house built, which was destroyed by fire just fifty years later.

Coles II served as surveyor of roads from his home at Green Mountain east to the Hardware River, and he corresponded and did business regularly with Thomas Jefferson. In fact, Coles gave Jefferson and his family refuge when they fled Tarleton's raid during the Revolutionary War.[7]

Edward Coles, son of John Coles II, was born at Enniscorthy and rose to prominence when he worked for President James Madison and then became governor of

Illinois. Perhaps Edward Coles's most long-lasting legacy, however, is that he renounced slavery and manumitted his nineteen slaves after taking them to safety in Illinois, where they would not be subject to the harsh laws applied to free people of color in Virginia during this time.

Although the original Enniscorthy house burned in 1839, a new plantation house that went by the same name was built around 1850 by Julianna Coles, the widow of John Coles II. The house is held in private ownership today and was remodeled in the early twenty-first century.

In 1796, John Coles II had Woodville, now known as "Old Woodville," built for his son Walter. When the family sold Old Woodville to the Shaw family, they built a new home by the same name nearby (at what is now the intersection of Porters and Esmont Roads).

In the late 1800s, the Coles family reacquired the original Woodville house, and it remained in their family well into the latter part of the twentieth century. Both homes are still standing and in wonderful condition, and the newer Woodville house is a thriving bed and breakfast.

Estouteville Plantation was built around 1827 by John Coles III on the same land as a home that went by the name Calycanthus. (The hill on which Estouteville now stands is still recorded as Calycanthus Hill in some records.) The house was designed and construction led by James Dinsmore, Thomas Jefferson's master carpenter. By one account, a former slave house has been converted into a tenant house on the property. Today the house still stands among tall trees at the top of the hill, near the intersection of Plank Road and Frys Path.

Estouteville house
(Photograph by Frances Benjamin Johnston, Carnegie Survey of the
Architecture of the South, Library of Congress, Prints and Photographs
Division, LCCN 2017889912, https://lccn.loc.gov/2017889912)

Tallwood Plantation was built in 1803 for John Coles II's son Tucker Coles (1782–1861). The plantation stayed in the Coles family until 1897, when Peyton Skipwith Coles (1853–?) sold the farm to a gentleman from Missouri. The home is now owned by the Van Clief family.

Coleswood, the final Coles property in the area, was constructed in 1903 by Peyton Skipwith Coles after he sold Tallwood and sits, still, between the Enniscorthy property and Tallwood, off Green Mountain Road.

Elizabeth Coles Langhorne (1909–2004)

Elizabeth Coles Langhorne, "Betty" to those who knew her, grew up at Coleswood, one of the plantation houses built for her ancestors and one of the twelve she documents in her book *A Virginia Family and Its Plantation Houses*. Langhorne authored several other books, including *Monticello: A Family Story*, which one reviewer says presents "a private Jefferson that rings true."[8]

Langhorne was also the cofounder of the Virginia Center for the Creative Arts in Amherst County, one of the most prestigious retreats for writers and other artists in the nation. Additionally, she founded the Vieques Conservation and Historical Trust in Puerto Rico, an organization dedicated to the preservation of the island's culture and natural resources.

By all accounts, Langhorne was a warm and vibrant force of life. She attended President Roosevelt's first inauguration and met her husband Harry Forsyth Langhorne while flying her own plane, *Our Betsy*.

To manage all these holdings, which included thousands of acres of land, the Coles family enslaved at least 329 people, according to the slave census of 1850; and by 1860, the census lists at least 429 people as enslaved to them.

These numbers indicate a significant level of wealth, of course, but also a level of comfort on the part of the family, since this number of enslaved people would have provided not only a sizable labor force for agriculture but also a staff to attend to all household needs, from cooking to cleaning to caring for the children.

In Esmont today, many of the African American families of this area can, in all likelihood, tie their presence in Southern Albemarle to their ancestors' survival and perseverance under the slave system on the Coleses' family plantations. The history of the Coles in Esmont is not only written in buildings but also lives on in many Esmont residents.

Canaan Plantation (now known as Liberty Corner)

Adjoining the communities currently known as Chestnut Grove and Porter's, the Canaan Plantation once sat, a property of 918 acres owned by Mathew M. Harris. The land was first bought by his father, Capt. John Harris of nearby Mountain View Plantation (located near Secretarys Sand Road), who made the purchase from another plantation owner, Wilson Cary Nicholas of Mount Warren, south of Esmont and on the James River.

According to extensive Harris family records, gathered by historian Sam Towler, Mathew M. Harris held a number of families in slavery, including people with surnames that still exist in the Chestnut Grove and Porter's communities, most prominently the surname of Carey. (Towler asked whether the surname Carey might have derived from the name Cary—i.e., Wilson Cary Nicholas—but definitive proof of such a connection is not likely to be discovered, given the nature of slavery and its lack of formal records about enslaved people.)[9]

Mount Warren Plantation

South of Canaan, along the James River, stood Mount Warren Plantation, home of Wilson Cary Nicholas, grandson of George Nicholas (1685–1734), who had received the original land grant for the acreage along the river in 1729. Wilson Cary Nicholas (1761–1820) studied law at William & Mary and eventually went on to become both a senator and a representative in the US Congress before becoming the governor of Virginia from 1814–16.

Wilson Cary Nicholas
(Reproduced by permission from the Library of Virginia)

Around 1793, at the mouth of Ballinger Creek, the town of Warren grew up by the landing that Nicholas had built to facilitate shipment of his wheat. Here, the town included a gristmill run by Robert Carter Nicholas (Wilson Cary's father), two other mills, a tobacco-inspection warehouse for Nicholas's crop, a distillery owned by Samuel Shelton, Jacob Kinney's Stone Tavern, a blacksmith shop, some homes (including the Wingfield Place, built in 1789 and owned by Charles Wingfield, an elder at nearby Ballenger Church), and a ferry. Given that the James River and Kanawha Canal passed through this area, making conveyance to Richmond possible and expedient, Warren held prominence as a major shipping destination until it was supplanted by Scottsville around 1820.[10]

The ferry landing at Warren is still visible along the canal at the mouth of Ballinger Creek. Above it, Mount Warren sits on the bluff overlooking the river, just as it always has, safe from the James's intermittent floods but with close access to the transport for goods and people that its waters gave.

Esmont Plantation

When Charles Cocke bought 1,184 acres from Rezin Porter in 1814, the land is recorded as being upon and contiguous to Green Mountain, adjacent to the Coles's property at Enniscorthy. On this land, in 1816, Cocke had his plantation house built; and by 1820, according to the US census from that year, he enslaved forty-two people at the plantation.

Esmont Plantation house

Roger MacBride (1929–1995)

In 1968, Esmont Plantation was bought by Roger MacBride, an attorney, politician, writer, and television producer.

MacBride and writer Rose Wilder Lane, daughter of Laura Ingalls Wilder (the author of the famous Little House on the Prairie and Little House series), became close. Many who knew MacBride said that he considered Lane his adopted grandmother and mentor. He also served as her attorney.

On Lane's death, MacBride was named her legal heir and executor, and he received her estate, including copyright ownership of all of the Little House books. MacBride would go on to write three additional titles in the book series as well as coproduce the *Little House on the Prairie* television show that was based on the books.

As a politician, MacBride first served in the Vermont House of Representatives in 1962; and after moving to Virginia, he became aligned with the Libertarian Party upon throwing his electoral vote from the Republicans to the Libertarians in 1972. This action brought him to the attention of the Libertarian Party, and in 1976, MacBride received their nomination for president. While living in Esmont, he ran against Gerald Ford and Jimmy Carter in that campaign and achieved .03 percent of the U.S. popular vote.

According to author Jan Karon, who owned the plantation for some time in the late twentieth century, its name may have come from the phrase "east of the mountains"—in other words, "est-mont," which is fitting since the property sits east of both Green Mountain and the Blue Ridge Mountains a bit further west. However, Cocke left no record for why he chose that particular name, so we cannot be sure of the origin.

Cocke sold the plantation in 1848, and it passed through a series of owners until bought in the 1890s by industrialists John and Henry Lane, whose business investments would help form the Village of Esmont at the turn of the twentieth century.

The plantation moved through several more hands after the Lanes owned it. In the late twentieth century, author Jan Karon had the plantation house fully restored to its original design, and it is still owned and maintained by a private owner today.

Other Plantations in Esmont

In addition to the Coleses' family plantations, Canaan, Mount Warren, and Esmont, a number of other plantations and smaller farms existed in the area:

- Morrisena Farm was constructed in 1750 for the Morris family and is still owned by the Morrises today.
- River Lawn Plantation was built in 1765 for Col. Joseph Joplin.[11]
- Seven Oaks Plantation was built in 1785 for Benjamin Childress (1764–1852) on 2,200 acres near what is now Mount Zion Methodist Church.
- Oakland Plantation (later Donegal) was built in 1806 for the Rives family.
- Monticola Plantation was built in 1853 for Daniel James Hartsook.[12]

The owners of these places—as well as the communities of Africans and African Americans they enslaved—knew each other, perhaps worshipped together, and worked together. In that way, Esmont has been a community of farmers for more than three hundred years, and the foundations of this rural, agricultural community were set in the system of slavery. That system informs how life is lived in Esmont for everything from the churches to the schools, to the road paths, to the communities themselves, even today.

VILLAGES

CHURCHES

ONCE EUROPEAN SETTLERS AND the Africans they enslaved began arriving in Virginia, they started to establish churches. Many of these congregations were part of the Church of England, but other denominations—namely Congregational and Baptist—formed in the area of Esmont too. In particular, Baptists—who believed in adult baptism instead of the baptism of infants and children, as did the Church of England—organized a number of key communities in and around Esmont. Many of these churches, of all denominations, still exist today.

Ballenger Church

The first church of record in the area was Ballenger Church (ca. 1750), which was located on the James River Road, between the communities of Porter's and Warren. It was part of Saint Anne's, the southernmost of Albemarle's two

Anglican parishes. The first rector of Saint Anne's was Rev. Robert Rose, who was followed by Rev. William Camp, Rev. John Ramsay, Rev. Charles Clay, and then Rev. Isaac Darnielle.[13]

According to records at the Albemarle Charlottesville Historical Society, Ballenger became a Baptist church sometime in the late eighteenth or early nineteenth centuries. The church membership rosters give its name as Ballenger Creek Baptist with its address as the town of Warren. In these records, we find that Charles Wingfield is listed as an elder, and prominent White families, with names including Hamner, Jefferson, Morrison, and Morris, served as deacons.

On the 1835 membership roster, the number of White members is listed as 57 and the number of "colored" members as 144, meaning that the church membership was almost 60 percent Black and, presumably, largely comprised of people enslaved by the White membership. In an August 1855 record of membership reported by the Albemarle Baptist Association annual meeting at Mount Shiloh Baptist Church in Nelson County, the membership consists of 53 White members and 238 "colored" members.

These numbers are fairly representative of Baptist church-membership demographics in the years preceding the Civil War. After Emancipation, Black Baptists often left—or were forced to leave—to form their own congregations. It's not an uncommon sight, even today, to find a Black Baptist church just up the road from a White Baptist church because, during the colonial and antebellum periods, Black people and White people attended church together.

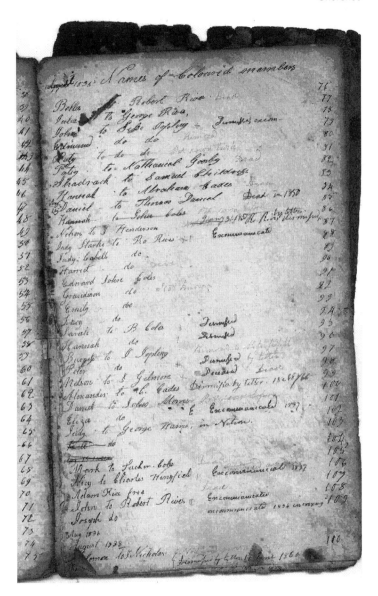

Ballenger Creek Baptist Church 1851 membership list
(Courtesy of the Albemarle Charlottesville Historical Society)

The Ballenger Creek Baptist Church records also list the names of all the "colored" members and their status (free or enslaved) as well as the names of their enslavers. While most Black individuals are listed by first name only, a few surnames are given: George Crofford, who is listed as enslaved to E[lizabeth] Coles; Susan Scott, a free woman who in 1835 is listed as deceased; Judy Starke and Judy Cabell, who are listed as enslaved by Robert Rives; Tom Malay, who is deceased but was enslaved by John Coles in 1846; Nancy Slaughter, who is listed as enslaved by Julia Coles, also in 1846; Lucy Jackson, who is listed as enslaved by Tucker Coles in 1856; and Edmund Mayo, a "free man of color."[14]

Ballenger Creek Baptist continued to operate until the mid-nineteenth century, and the reason for the church's dissolution is not clear. However, sometime in the late nineteenth century, the church was converted into a private residence; and according to some records, it has since been torn down.

In approximately 1762, the glebe of Saint Anne's Parish, a property of some four hundred acres, was bought by Samuel Jordan and Patrick Napier, church wardens, to support the parish. This land was located south of Porter's Precinct and is now marked by a historical marker that reads,

> In 1762 the vestry of St. Anne's Parish purchased from William Burton 400 acres here for the residence and lands of the rector of the parish, established in 1745. This glebe was so used almost until the dissolution of the old parish. It was sold in 1779 to Joseph Cabell.[15]

The Cabell family was a prominent family in the area, with vast holdings in nearby Nelson County. Joseph Cabell sat on the Virginia House of Burgesses and then as a senator in the new Virginia government. The glebe land in Southern Albemarle was but one piece of his vast land holdings.

Mount Zion Methodist Church

In 1828, Benjamin Childress (1765–1852), owner of Seven Oaks Plantation, had the people he enslaved build a log meetinghouse on his property along what is now Dawsons Mill Road. In later years, the congregation constructed a brick church, and when that building began to fail, the present-day wooden structure was built.

Mount Zion Methodist Church

A large cemetery, begun in 1853, sits to the north side of the church, on land donated by Childress and then added to by the owner of Canaan, a Mr. Earle.[16]

The church is still a functioning congregation to this day, with descendants of the Childress family and the Dawson family still active and fervent members. (Mildred Childress, Benjamin's granddaughter, married John Stanley Dawson of nearby Cool Springs Farm.) The church meets each Sunday and hosts a wide and welcome homecoming in the spring.

Sharon Baptist Church

Just west of Mount Zion sits Sharon Baptist Church, founded in 1852 and located in the community now known as Chestnut Grove. This church also has a small cemetery adjacent to the church building, where people have been buried since at least the early twentieth century.

Sharon Baptist Church
(Photograph by Dave Johnson, Friends of Esmont)

New Hope Baptist Church

In 1865, New Hope Baptist Church was built as a log cabin on land near where the church sits now. The first offering at that building brought in $3.77, and this money provided the down payment for the property where the church is currently located on Porters Road, just south of Irish Road. The first pastor at the church was Joseph Cary.

On the original land, the church structure has been reconstructed twice, once because it was condemned and once because of fire. The current church was erected in 1940. A cemetery lies next to the church building; and another cemetery, for nearby New Green Mountain Baptist Church, formed out of New Hope, is adjacent. Over two hundred people are buried in New Hope's cemetery, with the earliest graves dating from the 1890s.

The church still meets regularly, with a thriving membership of more than two hundred people.

Chestnut Grove Baptist Church

In 1868, Chestnut Grove Baptist Church was established. The church's first building was a log structure; and then, in 1906 and again in 1965, as the church's cornerstone states, the church building was reconstructed.

It is likely that this congregation was formed by people who had been enslaved at some of the nearby plantations, such as Canaan and those held by the Coles family, especially since some of the early members—for instance, Nicey Ann Coles, whose great-great-granddaughter Regina Rush was born in the area—may have carried the names of their former enslavers into modern times.

Nicey Ann Coles Rush Moseley
(~1823–~1880)

The first records we have of Nicey Ann Coles are on an inventory of people enslaved by Robert Rives Sr. of Oak Ridge in Nelson County. There, she is listed as valued at $600 for herself and two of her children, Betsy and Sam. Other records from Oak Ridge indicate that she and her long-standing partner Isham may have had as many as fourteen children, including Nathan, William, Ella, Cecilia, Louisiana, Lucy, Isham, Neverson, and Fleming.

When Rives Sr. died in 1845, Nicey and Isham were moved to South Warren, another of the family plantations owned by Robert Rives Jr. As Nicey and Isham's great-great-granddaughter Regina Rush notes, "Not much is known about the Rush family's day-to-day existence at South Warren."[17] But records indicate that, in January 1851, Nicey gave birth to Regina Rush's great-grandmother Ella and, that same month, Nicey tried to escape. We do not know the reasons Nicey ran, and her attempted escape is noted in Rives's ledger only with a statement that he paid H. D. Robertson for apprehending her.

While Isham fades from history by 1868, we do have far more information about Nicey, thanks to exhaustive research by her great-great-granddaughter Regina. On September 18, 1868, Nicey and Paul Moseley were married at the newly built Chestnut Grove Baptist Church, exactly seventeen years from the day that Rives recorded Nicey's recapture.

In 1870, Nicey was forty-seven and living in Warren with her husband Paul, her stepson Paul Jr., seven of her children, and her granddaughter, Sophronia. By 1880, Nicey had moved closer to Scottsville. Since Nicey does not appear on the 1900 census, it appears she died sometime between 1880 and 1900 and is, presumably, buried at Chestnut Grove Baptist Church, although her grave there is not marked.[18]

Nicey Ann Coles Rush and Paul Moseley were married at Chestnut Grove Baptist on September 20, 1868, not long after the church was built. The Rush family is still prominent and active at Chestnut Grove Baptist Church and the surrounding community.

The church thrives in the Chestnut Grove community of Esmont today, with services every Sunday.

Mount Alto Baptist Church

On the western side of Esmont sits Mount Alto Baptist Church. The church was formed in 1882 under the leadership of H. Allen and has operated continuously ever since.

Nearby, in 1890, the members of that community constructed a school, called Mount Alto School, for African American children. It cost $700 to build. The first year, nineteen students attended, and the school operated at least through the 1930s.[19]

Mount Alto Baptist Church
(Photograph by Dave Johnson, Friends of Esmont)

Adjacent to the church building is a cemetery with more than forty graves, most dating from the twentieth century.

Sand Road Baptist Church

In 1883, Sand Road Baptist Church was formed on the north side of Esmont, near Alberene, and still holds services regularly. Next to the church is a cemetery with over seventy graves.

Just down the road, around 1930, the Sand Road School was built for African American children. The building stood into the twenty-first century but was then demolished.

New Green Mountain Baptist Church

New Green Mountain Baptist Church was organized in 1896 on Porters Road, just north of Irish Road. The congregation met in a small wooden structure until 1946. At that time, it became clear a new building was needed, and the first church structure was demolished. The new building was begun in 1948; and improvement continued for many decades, as church needs changed and funds became available. The church still meets every Sunday and is a vibrant, thriving congregation.

South of the church, near New Hope Baptist Church, the cemetery for New Green Mountain consists of over 180 graves, the earliest of which date from the late nineteenth century.

New Green Mountain Baptist Church

Saint Stephen's Episcopal Church

Saint Stephen's Episcopal Church, on Esmont Road, was constructed in 1914 under the leadership of the Rev. E. B. Meredith, using Carpenter Gothic style. The interior is tongue-and-groove boards laid on the diagonal, creating a rustic cathedral-like effect, and the building seats about ninety people. The church cemetery, administered by the Christ Church Glendower Cemetery Committee, adjoins the church.

Over the years, Saint Stephen's has played a major role in the Village of Esmont. During the village's heyday, the church had its own vestry, ECW (Episcopal Church Women), altar guild, and Sunday school.

As the village declined, so did the church programs. Eventually, the building was closed, with only a single annual service, until the church was reopened in 1995.

The future looks bright for Saint Stephen's Church.

Saint Stephen's Episcopal Church

Churches in rural places are always central. They are social networks and social systems. They provide support where governmental services fail, and they offer respite and sanctuary in times of need. The churches of Esmont have certainly served the community this way and continue to do so. Esmont's churches have been a crucial part of forming community organizations like the local health center and the School Leagues, and they continue to be a core aspect of life in this rural and thriving community.

SCHOOLS

IN RURAL VIRGINIA, EDUCATION was usually a communal effort. Most communities had local elementary schools to which young students walked each day. These structures typically consisted of one or two rooms, with a teacher in each room. Often, they included potbelly stoves, fueled by wood or coal, that many times the children came early to start in order to warm the building.

Esmont was no different, with small elementary schools in most of its various communities just after the Civil War, and two high schools as well, one for White students and one for Black students.

By 1878, the first school in the area opened. The African American community at Porter's Precinct had built a log school for the community's children on land donated by

John Lane, a member of the Lane family who would help to form the Village of Esmont. Lane was the first teacher at the school. Soon after, in 1890, the school at Mount Alto Baptist Church was established.

In the very early twentieth century, perhaps by 1906, Hilltop School (now a residence on Boatwright Lane in the town of Esmont) was organized for the community's White students. The school was open for just a few years before becoming a residence for Jack Lane, son of Henry Lane of the Lane Furniture company and an early industrialist who helped develop Esmont Village.

Hilltop School
(Courtesy of Diane Pullaro)

Shortly after Hilltop School opened, the Men's and Women's School Leagues from Porter's Precinct formed. Around the same time, the Forsyths from Nydrie hall (constructed in 1898) funded the hiring of a teacher for Black students at the Loving Charity Lodge, now the Sons of

Esmont Lodge, just north of Irish Road on Porters Road. The Forsyths hired Rebecca Moore of New Orleans to teach in the school. An early description of the school notes that "it has two small windows, slab plank benches with no back rest and only the desk which was crudely formed."[20]

In 1910, the community of Chestnut Grove established a neighborhood school (Chestnut Grove School) near the Chestnut Grove Baptist Church, and some records indicate it was a church school. That term, however, likely just indicates that it was partially funded by the membership of the church, not that it offered religious education of any specific nature.

Chestnut Grove School operated well into the mid-twentieth century. Teachers there included Elsie Armistead, Geneva Lightfoot, Mary Scott, Isaac Scott, and Josephine Feggans.

Chestnut Grove School
(Photograph by Dave Johnson, Friends of Esmont)

By 1912, the Educational Board of Esmont (also known as the School League), a community organization of Black residents led by Benjamin F. Yancey, an educator, owned the deed to three acres of land on Porters Road, just south of Irish Road. Just three years later, the Esmont Colored School opened as the first high school for any students in the area, on land the Educational Board had purchased in the community of Porter's Precinct.

The building was a six-room structure and cost $4,000 to construct. Later, it became known as the Esmont High School.

Esmont High School class of 1943
(Reproduced by permission from the Scottsville Museum)

First row, left to right: Albert Henderson, Leona Waynes, Ida Johnson, Annie Mae Brown, James Copeland

Second row, left to right: Lawrence Moon, Jessie Johnson, Isaac D. Faulkner (Principal), Stanley Jordan, Francis Scott

Rebecca Monroe Jordan (1901–1999)

Rev. Rebecca Monroe Jordan was the pastor at South Garden Baptist Church and a teacher at the Esmont Colored School. She lived in the heart of Porter's Precinct, just two doors up from the B. F. Yancey Elementary School, with her husband General Jordan and their twelve children. She and General were married for over seventy years.

Rev. Jordan's ancestors were enslaved at Highland Plantation and carried the surname of their former presidential enslaver, James Monroe.

By 1922, Esmont School opened to elementary-age White students in the Village of Esmont, and that building still stands today, near Saint Stephen's Episcopal church off Esmont Road. Teachers at the school, which operated until 1962, included Mrs. H. Ward Jones, Mrs. A. A. Douglas, W. E. Hall, Felta Funkhouser, and Helen McMillan.

Esmont School
(Courtesy of the Albemarle County Public Schools)

Esmont's White, high-school-age students attended Scottsville School.

As the Black community continued to grow in population, so grew the need for another school for African American students; and thus, in approximately 1935, the community opened the "Little School," where students in kindergarten through fourth grade attended.

At the same time, Esmont High School (still a school only for African American students, since they were not allowed to attend high school with White students in Scottsville) began educating Black students in grades five through eleven. For many years, the graduations for the school alternated between New Hope Baptist and New Green Mountain Baptist Churches, recalls longtime Esmont resident Rosa Hudson.

In 1944, the Parent-Teacher League from Esmont High School purchased four acres adjacent to the land on which the existing high school sat, bringing the size of that total parcel to seven acres.

Black high school students from the area continued to attend Esmont High School until 1951, when Albemarle County consolidated the three Black high schools in the county (Esmont, Jefferson, and the Albemarle Training School). At that point, African American high school students from Esmont began going to school in Charlottesville, at Burley High School.

In 1960, B. F. Yancey Elementary School was built on the land occupied by Esmont High School. The school was named after Benjamin F. Yancey, the leader of the School League that helped establish the Black schools in the area. In the 1960s, the school became an integrated school for both

White and Black children of the area; and in 2017, B. F. Yancey Elementary was closed, despite much community protest. The building now serves as a community center.

Benjamin Franklin Yancey (~1870–1915)

Benjamin Franklin Yancey was a son of Albemarle, born in Howardsville to Fannie (Brown) and Spencer Yancey.

Yancey received his education at the Hampton Institute and then returned to Albemarle County to take his first teaching position at the Black Branch School, just north and east of present-day Keene. During that time, Yancey's dedication to the Esmont community—where his wife Harriet had been born and raised—grew; and in the effort to bring a school to Esmont, he began applying his fierce commitment to the education of African American children.

Yancey helped organize a men's group called the School League, and the following year a group of women also formed, all dedicated to the purpose of establishing a school in Esmont. By 1913, the School League had purchased three acres of land on Porters Road; and eventually, that land became the home of the Esmont Colored School (later called Esmont High School).

Yancey and his wife both taught at the school, and when Yancey died in 1915, at the age of just forty-four, his wife continued to teach there. His daughter May would become a teacher in the school as well, and his son Roger went on to law school and became a judge in New Jersey.

Some forty-five years after his death, Yancey's legacy was still being felt in the vibrant educational system he helped found in Esmont, so the community decided to name the new elementary school after him. B. F. Yancey Elementary served the students of Esmont until it was closed in 2017.

Benjamin F. Yancey is buried in the New Hope Baptist Church Cemetery, near the school building that honors his enduring legacy.

In present-day Esmont, as of this writing, all students attend Scottsville Elementary, then Walton Middle School, and finally Monticello High School.

INDUSTRY

FOR MOST OF HISTORY, Esmont has been a rural community; but for about seventy years—from roughly 1884 until 1950—Esmont became a small city because of two important geographical features: soapstone and slate. The Monacans had known about soapstone for eons, but it was only in the late nineteenth century that the impressive seam of the soft rock became known to the rest of the world; and soon thereafter, the infrastructure that gave access to soapstone provided the opportunity to also mine the area's slate deposits.

According to an article published in *Scientific American* in 1896, the business of quarrying Esmont's soapstone began when "one day a horseman appeared riding slowly, with observant eyes, a man of experience, an expert in soapstone. Here he found outcropping a vein of soapstone, the finest in the world."[21]

Other versions of this story about James Serene, one of the founders of the Albemarle Soapstone Company, include that he saw the stone when passing by during the Civil War or that he noticed it on a visit to relatives in the area. But most likely, he came to the area seeking soapstone because he and his father-in-law owned a soapstone business in New York, and soapstone was a hot commodity at the time.[22]

Esmont quarry site
(Photograph by Peggy Purvis Denby, Friends of Esmont)

Because the stone does not corrode from acid, does not effectively conduct heat, is remarkably strong, and is relatively soft and therefore easy to quarry, soapstone hit a boom during the Victorian period at the end of the nineteenth century. It was used in medical facilities and jewelry shops, where the chemicals could corrode other stone. It adorned the finest houses of the Northeast, where it formed lintels and bathtubs.

Thus, Serene had reason to be hunting for the stone; and given that people had been quarrying soapstone for centuries, using it for everything from ceremonial bowls to housewares, its presence in eastern Albemarle County was hardly a secret.

So it was that in 1883, James Serene and business partners John G. Porter and Selina Carroll (as proxy, it seems, for her husband Daniel) bought an almost-two-thousand-acre farm called Beaver Dam, along the creek by that same name (now a stream called Beaver Branch). There, they built a town—then called Johnson's Mill Gap or Beaver Dam but soon to take on the name of the stone, Alberene, a combination of "Albemarle" and "Serene"—complete with a company store, a school, a post office, a doctor's office, a barber shop, a boarding house for unmarried workers, and a massive mill for cutting the quarried stone.

As the company grew, the corporation built housing for employees, including the impressive and distinctive Alberene House, which today stands, with its turrets and porches, on what was then known as Maple Avenue. The "villages" of housing were given picturesque names like Dogtown, Stumptown, Quality Row, Gospel Hill, Church Hill, Sand Hill, and Carter's Field.[23] By 1900, over 250 men worked in the Alberene quarries and mill.

The company also constructed a massive barn to house the animals—mules and oxen—that were needed to haul the stone twice a day across muddy roads to North Garden, but this process was too slow to keep up with demand. Thus, Daniel Carroll decided to build a railroad. In 1895, the Alberene Railroad Company came into being, with C. D. Langhorne, local farmer, as president and Henry L. Lane as a principal stockholder.

The railroad's eleven-mile path was planned from Warren up Ballinger Creek to Esmont Plantation (purchased around this time by Henry Lane) before it circled around John Guthrie Hopkins's massive estate, Guthrie Hall (built in 1901), and finally reached the town of Alberene. It took nearly a year for right-of-way to be granted by local farmers, and it was only by order of condemnation that Andrew J. Dawson (of Cool Springs Farm) and John Tompkins were forced to sell their land.

**Surviving railway trestle supports
constructed with soapstone blocks**
(Photograph by Dave Johnson, Friends of Esmont)

Once right-of-way was secured, Lane Brothers and Company, owned by John and Henry Lane, put crews to work, beginning at Alberene and then later at Warren. Most of the line was constructed by hand with explosives only put to use when necessary.

In March or April 1898, the railroad began running; but despite much excitement and conjecture about the opening in local papers, no one seems to have recorded the actual date the railroad started operations.

It ran routinely, with only one accident, but a horrible one. In January 1901, train 57 turned over while going north above Esmont, and the engineer, William H. McCartney, was killed. The fireman, Charles H. Clay, was also badly injured; but as one historian notes, "Conductor Luck lived up to his name and escaped almost without a scratch."

The gentlemen of Albemarle Soapstone Company also expanded into a number of other industries; but in Esmont, one of their ventures was to have long-lasting consequences, for both good and ill, for the people of that community. In 1899, Henry Lane, George Bostwick, and Daniel Carroll formed Carbolane Slate Company (another cutesy title created from their surnames), a slate-quarrying company that harvested the green slate Lane found on his property at Esmont Plantation. Carbolane Slate opened in 1899 but closed its doors by 1910.

Blue Ridge Slate, another slate-mining company—operating on the west side of the village and often called the "Dust Plant" by residents—milled slate for many years. On some days, remembers Peggy Purvis Denby, the dust was so thick that they had to turn on the lights in their family home before dark just to be able to see.

Eventually, the state ordered that Blue Ridge Slate abate the massive dust its operation produced; but given the costs of the necessary modifications, the company chose to close the plant instead. The blight of white powder that had dusted the town and its inhabitants for decades ended. Still, this dust made many, many residents of Esmont sick and was responsible for a great number of deaths in the community.

Soapstone quarrying continued far longer than slate quarrying did, although it too was on again, off again as advancements in quarrying technology made it possible to harvest more and more of the stone. In 1909, twenty-five years after first opening, Albemarle Soapstone closed its doors for the first time, after having mined all the stone it could harvest, and then the mill for shaping the stone closed in 1916. But later that same year, Virginia Alberene Corporation was formed and employed 650 men.

Just a few years after Lane and Carroll began quarrying soapstone in Alberene, James Foster and Max Wiehle began a similar venture, Virginia Soapstone Company, in nearby Schuyler, building a state-of-the-art mill and encouraging the growth of a town much like Esmont Village. By 1900, Virginia Soapstone employed 175 people.

However, the company struggled financially, having sunk all its capital into the mill and a railroad from Rockfish to Schuyler without a plan to market its product. Albemarle Soapstone, in contrast, had plenty of capital but was already running low on material to serve its market. James Serene opposed the purchase of Virginia Soapstone; but when he died from pneumonia on a trip to New York, his partner Daniel Carroll purchased controlling stock in

Virginia Soapstone from Max Wiehle's family after Wiehle's death, also from pneumonia.

By 1904, Albemarle Soapstone and Virginia Soapstone merged into a single company, retaining the Albemarle Soapstone name, with Daniel Carroll as president and James Foster as vice president. Quarrying at Alberene ended about 1910, but the mill remained active, working stone from Schuyler, until about 1916.

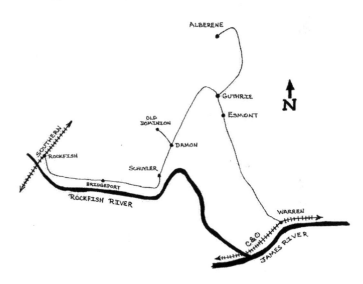

Service area of the Nelson and Albemarle Railway
(Reproduced by permission from Garth G. Groff, *Soapstone Shortlines: Alberene Stone and its Railroads* [Charlottesville: Drop Leaf Press, 1991])

The company needed a way to facilitate transport between its two operations; and in 1903, the Nelson and Albemarle Railway Company was chartered. The railway included ten stops from Warren up to Alberene, including the Esmont Depot, which was constructed by the Lane brothers. Tapscott Lumber Yard was located on the rail yard in Esmont Village and also used the railway to carry its pulpwood and railroad ties from the 1940s on. It was a busy operation.

Tapscott Lumber Lane headquarters
(Courtesy of Edna Tapscott Anderson)

Far left: Tucker Tapscott

Eventually, the Schuyler Railway, a line built by Foster and Wiehle to move materials from Rockfish to Schuyler, joined the Nelson and Albemarle line; and thus, Esmont became the central hub of a three-pronged spoke of short rail lines serving the quarries of the region.

These rails provided more than transport of goods, however. They were also heavily used passenger trains, carrying people from the Southern Railway at Rockfish (now the Norfolk Southern line) north and east to Schuyler, then to Esmont, on up to Alberene, and down to Warren. The depot served as a prominent stop for travelers and sat at the heart of Esmont Village.

Esmont Depot
(Reproduced by permission from Garth Groff;
photograph by Charles Arnold, the Garth Groff Collection)

The passenger service lasted from 1906 until 1950, when supplanted by automobile travel. The last passenger train ran on February 4, 1950, and collected over seventeen dollars in fares, more than had come in on the line for months. Operators that day were longtime railroad men: John C. Mayo, the engineer, had started when the Nelson and Albemarle line began in 1903; Conductor H. L. Drumheller had come to the railroad in 1918; Brakeman J. Critzer, in 1919; and Fireman A. L. Drumheller, in 1920.[24]

Just as Esmont came into its own, the people who had helped launch the town into an economic center, John and Henry Lane, turned their attention elsewhere. By 1908,

John Lane had begun building the town that would become Altavista, about eighty miles southwest of Esmont. By 1912, he had founded what would become the still-thriving business known as Lane Furniture. He remained the vice president and a stockholder in the Nelson and Albemarle Railway until 1920, but at that point his name disappears from the company records.[25]

The prosperity brought by the soapstone and slate mills, and the access brought by their railroads, created a time of great economic boom in the communities of Esmont. By 1925, one thousand employees worked at thirty-five quarries in the Esmont and Schuyler areas.[26] Given that the population of all Albemarle County was just under 27,000 in 1930, this means that over 3 percent of the people in the county were employed at quarries in Esmont.

The stock market crash of 1929 and the subsequent depression of the 1930s brought hard times to the industries of the Esmont region. Workers were laid off. Operations cut back, and paychecks were scarce.

But even then, Esmont was a vibrant community with two town centers (not including nearby Alberene, Schuyler, and Keene) serving these quarries and the railroads that fed them.

The quarries continued harvesting stone on and off for decades, as various demands for the stone—including a contribution of sinks and countertops for the Manhattan Project facilities in Tennessee and Washington State—waxed and waned. But the need for the railroad lines themselves eventually disappeared altogether in the 1960s, when the tracks were abandoned, and the golden age of Esmont's industry faded away.

The last train traveled the Nelson and Albemarle Railway on January 5, 1963, on a run from Schuyler to Warren via Esmont, where it picked up three loads of pulpwood from the Tapscott Lumber Yard (which moved operations to Warren when the rail service ended). A year later, the Esmont Depot was disassembled, marking the end of Esmont Village's economic boom.

Alberene soapstone is still quarried today in Schuyler. A company by the name of Polycor now owns the Alberene quarries and mines stone that is used in countertops and other applications around the world.

Perhaps most poetically, some of the soapstone quarries at Schuyler have been turned into beautiful gardens that feature native plants. The Quarry Gardens at Schuyler, created by Armand and Bernice Thieblot, have returned the quarries of the area to a natural form that might well harken back to the first days of mining by the Monacans and where local residents can visit the history of their land's gifts in all their forms.

COMMERCE

THE ESMONT AREA HAS been home to what those of us who know rural places call "towns," and those of us from more urban environments might think of as "crossroads," since the days when European American and African American people first came to live here. These small communities—Warren, Porter's Precinct, Chestnut Grove, and Esmont Village—were and still are hubs of life in this rural region; but as is often the case in American history, the commercial lives of these places were typically short lived, lasting only a few decades, until larger or more easily accessible sites became prominent.

The first of these villages was Warren, at the very southern end of the area now covered by the Esmont zip code on the James River. As noted earlier, Warren was a small town from the late eighteenth century until the early nineteenth century, when the wide, flat waters of the James at Scottsville became the center of commerce for most of southern Albemarle County.

Porter's Precinct

After the end of the Civil War and the enactment of the Emancipation Proclamation, the community of Porter's Precinct (often called simply "Porter's") became an established place, first appearing on the Green Peyton map of 1867 as "Porters." It formed around the intersection of Irish Road, which connected Scottsville with the nearby town of Schuyler, and Porters Road, which tied Warren and the plantations on the James with the plantations of the Coles family at Woodville and those further north, toward Jefferson's Monticello.

Over the course of the years after slavery ended, the primarily African American community of Porter's included a gamut of businesses needed in any area: mechanics, beauticians, building contractors, midwives, barbers, farmers, upholsterers, restaurants (including Julia's Inn on Irish Road, where the food and the music were said to be stellar), blacksmiths, morticians, seamstresses, doctors and nurses, attorneys, ice harvesting services, musicians, judges, ministers, and shops such as Fred Thomas's store, where the sodas were cold and the jukebox lively when children stopped by after school.[27]

The community also had its own post office, at the corner of Irish and Porters Roads, for a brief period in the early twentieth century.

W. D. Ward (1907–1967)

Wardell D. Ward was the pastor of Union Baptist in Scottsville and Thessalonia Baptist in Fork Union, as well as Mount Pleasant Baptist Church in Keene, but he also served the Esmont community he called home as a carpenter. "Big Daddy," as the younger members of his family called him, was responsible, with the assistance of Lindsay Dorrier, for getting the streetlights approved on Porters and Irish Roads.

His kindness and generosity were so appreciated that, for many years, the building now known as the Odd Fellows Hall was called the "W. D. Ward Community Center" in his honor. Rev. Ward and his wife Julia Nelson Ward had eight children, including Nancy Luck, who for over twenty-six years served as the supervisor at the Yancey School Community Center, which originally met in the hall named for her father.

Tragically, Rev. Ward was killed in a car accident at the age of just sixty.

Currently, Brown's market, a gas station and convenience store at the intersection of Irish Road and Porters Road, is the only existing storefront in Esmont. Brown's has been actively serving the area for more than sixty years and was rumored as the home of the world's best chicken before owner Mike Brown moved his food operation to Charlottesville, where the chicken is still purportedly some of the best out there.

In addition to having had a thriving economic infrastructure, the people of Porter's Precinct were part and parcel of the many successful and diligent efforts to build and fund schools for African American children in their community. Today, Porter's is home to the Yancey School Community Center (housed in the former B. F. Yancey

Elementary School), where the longest-lasting senior center in Albemarle meets every Tuesday and Thursday.

The center also hosts Piedmont Virginia Community College classes, a food pantry, and other community programs, and is the polling place for a large swath of southern Albemarle County. Across the street, Simpson Park provides outdoor recreational space for children, families, and others who wish to spend time at the water park, playground equipment, or picnic facilities.

Many of the residents of Porter's, in addition to running their own businesses over the years, have worked for the quarries in the area or were employed by the Van Clief family, who purchased Woodville and several other Coles properties. In particular, Lorraine Paige worked for several decades as Mrs. Van Clief's personal secretary.

Daniel G. Van Clief (1925–1987)

Whenever anyone asks about the people who have done good by Esmont, Daniel G. Van Clief's name comes up. Danny, as he was known, came to Esmont from New York when his parents, Ray and Margaret, purchased Nydrie—a neo-Gothic estate just north of the Village of Esmont—and established a horse farm there in 1928.

Lorraine Paige, Mrs. Van Clief's secretary for several decades, recalls that the Van Clief family employed twenty to thirty people at the farm, with many people working in the horse barns and others working in the house in various capacities. Ben Paige also worked as the family chauffeur and butler for many, many years, and the Paiges and their children often traveled with the Van Cliefs and their four sons.

Van Clief served in the Fourth Infantry of the US Army during World War II and was in the first wave of soldiers to storm Utah Beach when he was just nineteen years old. When he came back from the war, his plans to attend college were put aside as he began to work at Nydrie with his parents.

Danny Van Clief married Margaret Robertson—"Peggy," as many knew her—and she was a beloved member of the Esmont community all her life. She worked with many organizations, including the American Cancer Society and the garden club. Danny served in the Virginia House of Delegates for three terms, where he was very proud to hold Thomas Jefferson's seat.

Shay Booth, a longtime resident of Esmont, remembers fondly that the Van Clief family would allow the town to borrow Nydrie's fire engine in emergencies, since the town itself did not have a fire company. Danny's son D. G. recalls that his father gladly lent the fire engine and his farm crew to serve as firefighters because he loved the Esmont community deeply. "If he had to choose," D. G. says of his father, "his commitment was always to Virginia and then to Southern Albemarle."

Although the family had the massive Nydrie house demolished in the 1970s due to the costs of its upkeep, Danny and Peggy continued to live on the farmland for the rest of their lives. Mr. and Mrs. Van Clief are buried in a private family cemetery at Nydrie farm, where they are now, as ever, part of the fabric of life in Esmont.

While the commerce is no longer as robust in Porter's, the residents of that area have been there for generations and continue to build and support the social fabric of a very vibrant, very rich community with improvement associations and social activities. At present, a lively group of Porter's residents from the Yancey School Community Center regularly organizes activities, including a skate night, for the community.

Esmont Village

The Village of Esmont came into being sometime around the turn of the twentieth century, when first the quarries and then the railroads began to pass along the creek, which runs parallel to what is now Esmont Road. The town was founded when Henry Lane carved off the lower portion of his Esmont plantation acreage and gave the village the plantation's name. Given that Lane helped bring industry to Esmont, it seems fitting that the name of his home traveled down the road to the business center.

In 1900, one of the first businesses to open in the town center at Esmont was the grocery store now commonly known as the Purvis Store. It served the entire community of Esmont with not only groceries but also modern conveniences, such as one of the first telephones in the area and one of the only televisions around.

Original Purvis Store
(Reproduced by permission from the K. Edward Lay Collection)

Residents would come to use the phone at the store and could pick up messages too, and one resident, Kevin Rush, remembers catching *Hee Haw* there on Saturday nights. The store was built by the Wingfield family, who sold it to the Butler family, who then sold it to the Purvis (then Goff) family, who continued to operate it until 1989.

In 1902, the Esmont National Bank opened as one of only three national banks in the county of Albemarle. The bank building, which still stands in the center of Esmont Village, originally housed both the bank and the offices of the Lane Construction Company, which built the structure.

In time, the Esmont Post Office would open there, as would the offices of the village's physician, Dr. Early. Sadly, the bank fell victim to the Great Depression and closed in 1933 by unanimous vote of the stockholders.

Currently, one half of the lower floor of the building still holds the post office for the Esmont community. Judy Brochu-Blake served as the last official postmaster at the Esmont Post Office. When she retired in 2012, the term "postmaster" ceased in Esmont. Today, the employees there are called "clerks."

Currency issued from Esmont National Bank
(Courtesy of Judy Brochu-Blake)

William Heath (1908–1992)

William Payne Heath grew up in Esmont. His father, Reuben Lindsay Heath, was the station master at the Esmont Depot for over thirty-five years; and his mother, Emma Payne Heath, was the postmaster at the Esmont Post Office for many years as well. Their son William, or "Boog" as he was known to his family and friends, followed in his parents' footsteps of service.

Heath gave his time and energy to many of Esmont's most crucial institutions. In particular, he is remembered for the thirty-eight years he served as Esmont's postmaster. Additionally, he was the president of the Esmont Community League, master of the local Masonic lodge, a member of the Albemarle County Board of Zoning Appeals for over twenty-nine years, and a member of the vestry at Saint Stephens Episcopal Church for thirty-four years.

Heath was well known in Esmont for his role in bringing an end to the danger from the slate plant, the "Dust Plant" as most people in the area called it, when he appeared on the witness stand in court and slammed down a cloth bag full of white slate dust, covering everyone in the courtroom with the fine powder. The state soon ordered the plant to abate the dust, and the company decided to close instead. Heath's demonstration definitely proved his point.

Heath was married to Estelle Boyce Heath for sixty years, and they had three children, raised in the heart of Esmont Village as living embodiments of how much he loved and served his community.

In 1907, Steed's Store, owned and operated by C. C. Steed, began business as a general mercantile that sold everything from household goods to animal feed to dry goods. People of the community remember Mr. Steed as a quiet but kind man. He was always dressed in a shirt and tie, wearing round, wire-rimmed glasses, a distinctive mustache, and his ever-present sleeve protectors. The Steed's Store building still stands on Esmont Road, with its unique half-barrel roof and green siding.

Next door, the Esmont Inn, built around 1908, gave lodging to the town's visitors. It was an impressive building with a wide double porch. Sadly, the building burned down in the 1960s.

Pace's Store, at the far south end of the village (known as the "Bottom" to some of Esmont's residents), was built in 1910 and served as a gas station, with two pumps, a mechanic's shop, and a convenience store until well into the 1950s. The building is still standing at the intersection of Esmont Road and Paces Store Road.

Virginia Pace (1897–1969)

Virginia "Virgie" Pace and her husband John Pace were the purveyors of Pace's Store and Service Station at the south end of Esmont Village, along the short road that bears their name and connects the village with Irish Road, thus pointing west and east.

When Virgie Pace's sons were high school age, on Saturday evenings people came from Charlottesville and neighboring villages to the Pace home, next door to their store, and made music on the front porch. Her husband played a banjo, and others brought instruments and joined in. Minor Pace, one of Virgie's sons, played the violin and the banjo. People came from miles around, listened, and joined in with their instruments, enjoying the music on a Saturday night.

In 1911, Lane's Commissary, built by Henry Lane for the workers at his quarries, opened just down the street from the Esmont National Bank and across from the train depot. The second floor of the building served as the Lane company headquarters. Later, the store became a drugstore and, later still, a general merchandise store run by the Payne family. The Payne Store, as it came to be called, caught fire in 1996. The store was no longer functioning, but Mrs. Payne was still living in the family home in the rear when the fire broke out. Fortunately, she escaped the blaze safely.

Lane's store
(Photograph by Steven G. Meeks,
courtesy of the Albemarle County Historic Preservation Committee)

Other businesses thrived during the heyday of Esmont Village, including the Tapscott Lumber Yard, which harvested chestnut logs, perhaps from nearby Chestnut Grove, and shipped them on the Nelson and Albemarle Railway lines from its location in Esmont.

And the social life in the village was vibrant too. Across the railroad track from the Purvis Store sat a large baseball field, home of the Esmont recreational team. Shay

Booth, daughter of longtime Postmaster William "Boog" Heath, recalls that her father was quite the pitcher and catcher in the league, which boasted teams from Esmont, Howardsville, Scottsville, Columbia, and other areas. Kathryn Clerico, who also grew up in Esmont, recalls her mother talking about the field having been used for revivals and film viewings as well.

However, once the quarries began to close or pare back on operations and the railroads shut down, the economic infrastructure of Esmont Village, like that in nearby Porter's, began to fail. Sadly, with that decline came the deterioration of many buildings that made up the heart of Esmont. While some of these fine structures still stand, most are in various states of disrepair; but the hope of a number of residents is that they can be restored and rejuvenated for use by the community's citizens again.

Rosialee Coffey (1902–1972)

Esmont's most well-known psychic was Rosialee Coffey. She was born on a large farm on Irish Road, near Damon, where her father, George Harris, also had a wood mill. George Harris built several homes in the Village of Esmont, including the one that Coffey lived in and used as her office for her extensive following of people seeking to know their fortunes. Coffey's house is still standing next to the Purvis Store, and her granddaughter Valerie Holt Cox lives in that home today.

Despite the commercial decline, the residents of Esmont have continued to care for each other in formal and casual ways. In particular, the community organized to bring health care to Esmont, and the Esmont Health

Center began in the early 1970s. The first location for the center was in the Farmers Home on Porters Road, just across from New Hope Baptist Church; but within ten years, the practice outgrew that location.

In the mid-1980s, the center became part of the Central Virginia Health Services, and the Health Center Advisory Council, with Waltine Eubanks as president, purchased the land on which the newly named Southern Albemarle Family Practice now sits. It is a full-service medical center, providing family-practice and mental-health services for the citizens of Esmont and the surrounding communities.

Today, the commercial life of Esmont is primarily limited to small stores supplying convenience items—as Brown's market does—that keep residents from having to make more trips than necessary into Scottsville, where the nearest grocery store is located, or Charlottesville, where the nearest hospital and large commercial offerings can be found. One does wish that the town centers of Porter's and Esmont Village were still strong, both for convenience and for the sake of camaraderie and connection that such Main Streets provided to their communities.

Perhaps economic activity will one day return to the thriving vigor of the early twentieth century; but make no mistake, a dearth of commerce in Esmont today does not indicate any lack of life. These communities are "alive and kicking," as one resident says—just more quietly, perhaps, than they once were.

EPILOGUE

IT IS EASY TO miss the life and vigor of a place like Esmont if you are not paying attention. Most people who travel Irish Road (or Route 6, as it is often known) wouldn't even know Esmont existed if not for a road sign along the byway. It's not a locale with a thriving tourist attraction or a large shopping district. Wineries, which exist all around the area, haven't even found their way there yet. It's a quiet place.

But quiet does not mean silent, and it definitely does not mean dead or poor. Quiet is simply that—a place of respite and rest, a place that knows itself and does not need to flaunt that knowledge, even when it has much to brag about.

Everywhere in Esmont—in the churches and gathering spaces, in the groups that are hoping to restore buildings and build community services, in the stories that thrive in the Scottsville Museum and the Race & Place Oral History Project—people are remembering the stories of their community and crafting new stories for the generations to come. In Esmont, roots go deep and wide. They travel with the people who leave and with those who return. They live on in church homecomings and high school reunions. They are captured in the pages of family histories and community-center story collections.

Esmont is not a dead place. It's not a ghost town. Esmont is alive and rich in every way. As resident Waltine Eubanks says, "Esmont, the garden spot of the world: we grow people here."

Come visit and see for yourself. You'll be welcomed with open arms and lots of stories, stories of history and of the hope they bring.

A NOTE FROM FRIENDS OF ESMONT

DEAR READERS:

We sincerely hope you will enjoy this history of Esmont.

Friends of Esmont, Inc., was organized for the express purpose of bringing back to Esmont some of the spirit and vitality it had in earlier times but lost in the ensuing years. To serve that purpose, we felt it necessary to document and explain the history of our community so everyone could fully appreciate what we want to accomplish.

The end of an era began when the "Dust Plant" closed in the mid-1950s, and with it went the railroad, and with that went the depot. Our plan for the path left by the railroad tracks is to convert it to a walking and riding trail that runs from Simpson Park in Porter's Precinct to Alberene, so everyone can enjoy the beauty of the area while exercising. The depot will be remembered with a historical marker located on the original site, explaining the building's history.

The area where the "Dust Plant" stood will hopefully become accessible to those who enjoy natural trails, and the area alongside Ballinger Creek is a perfect place to establish a wetland for our feathered friends.

The former hub of activity in the village, Purvis Store, will once again be the hub as it is reclaimed into a variety of uses, including a grocery store, artists' booths, and the Esmont Museum and Visitors Center, while the shed next door is converted to a trailhead for those passing through on the trail.

Surely, visiting and enjoying these amenities and seeing the many renovated and restored houses in the village will lift everyone's spirits and bring back memories of what used to be. Then, Friends of Esmont, Inc., will have accomplished it mission.

—Friends of Esmont, Inc.

First Board of Directors for Friends of Esmont, Organized in 2018

Peggy Purvis Denby, *Chair*
Denise Bush, *Vice-Chair*
Don W. Jones, *Secretary*
Robbbyrda Preston, *Treasurer*
Judy Brochu-Blake, *Community Liaison*
Anna Boeschenstein, *Chair Trail Committee*
Mark Otis, *Consultant to Board*

ABOUT THE AUTHOR

Andi Cumbo-Floyd is a historian and writer with roots in Fluvanna County, just east on the James from Esmont. Her work includes *The Slaves Have Names* and *Steele Secrets*. She lives in Stanardsville, Virginia, another rural community with deep roots.

ACKNOWLEDGEMENTS

THERE WAS NO WAY to know the level of interest that existed, locally and beyond, in researching and documenting the history of Esmont, or that it would be overwhelming. What little had been documented led all to believe there was a rich history that needed to be told in oral stories and in writing before it was all forgotten.

Thanks to those such as Jan Karon and Garth Groff, who took the early first steps to preserve an important place and sense of time: Jan Karon's restoration of the house at Esmont Farm, from whence came the village, and Garth Groff's thorough history of area trains in his *Soapstone Shortlines*.

Many thanks to all the community members—Lorraine Paige, D. G. Van Clief, Rosa Hudson, Karl Bolden, Graham Paige, Jeffrey Hantman, Edward Brooks, Shay Heath Booth, Pat Healy, Nancy Miller, Mary Roy, Doug Bush, Jim Lewis, the members of the Esmont Community Senior Center, Dave Johnson, and many others—for their time, stories, and dedication to this history of Esmont.

Now, Friends of Esmont is expressing, in words and in deeds, their similar pride and love for the entire community and all that made it a real, fun, loving, and human place for everyone who lived and worked there.

The early discoverers of the slate and soapstone deposits could not have realized at the time what a gem they had found and what Esmont would become. All Friends of Esmont are pleased and grateful that they have participated in the modern-day polishing of what the gem led to.

*This history book has been funded in part by
Virginia Humanities, Preservation Piedmont,
and the Caplin Foundation of Fairfield, CT.*

NOTES

Monacan Settlements

1   Michael J. Klein, "The Transition from Soapstone Bowls to Marcey Creek Ceramics in the Middle Atlantic Region: Vessel Technology, Ethnographic Data, and Regional Exchange," *Archaeology of Eastern North America* 25 (1997): 143–158.

2   Jeffrey L. Hantman, *Monacan Millennium: A Collaborative Archaeology and History of a Virginia Indian People* (Charlottesville: University of Virginia Press, 2018).

3   Karenne Woods and Diane Shields, *The Monacan Indians: Our Story* (Amherst, VA: Monacan Indian Nation, 1999).

Land Grants – Eighteenth and Nineteenth Centuries

4   "About the Virginia Land Office Patents and Grants/ Northern Neck Grants and Surveys," Library of Virginia, accessed May 21, 2020, https://www.lva.virginia.gov/public/guides/opac/ lonnabout.htm#patents.

5   Eric W. Nye, "Pounds Sterling to Dollars: Historical Conversion of Currency," accessed March 20, 2020, https://www. uwyo.edu/numimage/currency.htm.

6   Many thanks to Robert Vernon and Michael Crabill for their extensive work mapping the land grants of the region.

Plantations

7   Thomas Jefferson Encyclopedia, "John Coles II," Thomas Jefferson Foundation, accessed May 21, 2020, https://www.monticello.org/site/research-and-collections/john-coles-ii.

8   Roy H. Tryon, review of Monticello: A Family Story, by Elizabeth Langhorne, Library Journal, 1987, out of print: partial review available at https://www.amazon.com/Monticello-Family-Story-Elizabeth-Langhorne/dp/091269758X.

9   For further information about Sam Towler's research on the enslaved community at Canaan, including a comprehensive and thoughtful PowerPoint presentation on that community, please contact Andi Cumbo-Floyd, andi@andilit.com.

10   K. Edward Lay, *The Architecture of Jefferson Country: Charlottesville and Albemarle County, Virginia* (Charlottesville: University of Virginia Press, 2000).

11   Papers of K. Edward Lay, Accession #12817, Special Collections Department, University of Virginia Library, Charlottesville, VA.

12   Erika Howsare, "April Abode: Monticola, a fine Albemarle estate, turns back the clock," *C-VILLE Weekly*, April 5, 2017, https://www.c-ville.com/april-abode-monticola-a-fine-albemarle-estate-turns-back-the-clock.

Churches

13   Edgar Woods, *Albemarle County in Virginia: giving some account of what it was by nature, of what it was made by man, and of some of the men who made it* (Charlottesville: The Michie Company, 1901).

14   Many thanks to Regina Rush, special collections reference coordinator at the University of Virginia's Albert and Shirley Small Special Collections Library and native to Chestnut Grove, for the recommendation of these documents, which are rich with historical information about African American people in the Esmont area: Ballenger Creek Church Records, Albemarle Charlottesville Historical Society, Charlottesville, VA.

15   Craig Swain, "The Glebe," Historical Marker Database, accessed May 21, 2020, https://www.hmdb.org/m.asp?m=29951.

16   "Mt. Zion Methodist Church, Esmont," Scottsville Museum, accessed May 21, 2020, https://scottsvillemuseum.com/church/homeCG1137CGCD2016.html.

17   Regina Rush, "The Rushes of Chestnut Grove: One Family's Journey from Slavery to Freedom," Scottsville Museum Newsletter 25 (Spring 2015): 4–6, 8.

18   Regina Rush, "The Rushes of Chestnut Grove."

19   "Mt. Alto Baptist Church," Scottsville Museum, accessed May 21, 2020, https://scottsvillemuseum.com/esmont/esmontchurches/mtaltobaptistchurch.html.

Schools
20   As cited in Albemarle County Public Schools, *Final Report of the Yancey Workgroup*, December 12, 2013: 9.

Industry
21   "Soapstone Quarries of Virginia," *Scientific American* LXXIV, no. 23 (June 6, 1896): 357, https://quarriesandbeyond.org/articles_and_books/pdf/soapstone_quarries_of_virginia_scientific_american_june_6_1896.pdf.

22   Garth G. Groff's extensive research on the soapstone quarries and their railroad short lines has been indispensable in constructing this story. You can find the much fuller history of this industry in his book *Soapstone Shortlines: Alberene Stone and Its Railroads*, published by Drop Leaf Press, Charlottesville, in 1991.

23   "A Brief History of Alberene as Remembered by Lurlein C. Kidd" (unpublished document, August 15, 1989), private collection.

24   "Railroad Fans Give N. and A. Record Haul on Final Day," Daily Progress (Charlottesville, VA), February 6, 1950.

25   Garth G. Groff, *Soapstone Shortlines: Alberene Stone and its Railroads* (Charlottesville: Drop Leaf Press, 1991).

26   Groff, *Soapstone Shortlines*.

Commerce
27   Many thanks to the Esmont Community Senior Center for their fine book *Days of Yesterdays*, which compiles the stories of the elders of the Porter's community.

Made in the USA
Columbia, SC
09 January 2021